TWENTY ESSENTIALS FOR THE
AIR FORCE
FIRST SERGEANT

HAMP LEE III

The contents of *Twenty Essentials for the Air Force First Sergeant* do not represent endorsement by the United States Air Force. Views are entirely representative of Hamp Lee III.

Twenty Essentials for the Air Force First Sergeant / Hamp Lee III — 2nd ed.

ISBN 978-1-940042-12-1

CONTENTS

I am a First Sergeant.

My job is people—everyone is my business.

I dedicate my time and energy to their needs;

Their health, morale, discipline and welfare.

I grow in strength

by strengthening my people.

My job is done in faith;

my people build my faith.

The Air Force is my life;

I share it with my people

I believe in the Air Force goal—

"We take care of our own."

My job is people—

EVERYONE IS MY BUSINESS

INTRODUCTION

I believe the role of the Air Force first sergeant is one of the most important positions in a military unit. As a focal point of enlisted readiness, morale, health, welfare, and discipline, the first sergeant is a principal advisor to the commander in preparing a mission-ready force. With such a critical position, it is important for a first sergeant to be adequately equipped with the necessary information and tools to successfully fulfill his or her role.

The first day I sat in my office as a first sergeant, I felt a little overwhelmed. I did not want to disappoint my commander or the Airmen. I wanted my unit to be confident in my abilities.

At the time of this writing, I am two years into my first sergeant special duty. I have had the honor of serving in a unit with one hundred Airmen and another with almost one thousand. Each unit has required me to take different approaches in making Airmen my business. Though I used different approaches in supporting each unit, there were foundational principles that helped me along the way.

As each first sergeant might address a situation differently, we share a common purpose in caring for Airmen. In supporting a diverse family of Airmen, it is important for a first sergeant to establish a solid foundation to help him or her lead successfully.

My purpose in writing *Twenty Essentials for the Air Force First Sergeant* is to help you be the best first sergeant possible. I want your units to be thankful to have you and sad to see you depart. I want you to leave a lasting impression that cannot easily be erased. I want you to inspire Airmen to reach their potential and cultivate a culture that embodies our Air Force Core Values and The Airman's Creed every day.

1

BUILDING BLOCKS

As I stated in the Introduction, I was a little overwhelmed on my first day as a first sergeant. But when I considered that I am a father, husband, brother, uncle, friend, confidant, Airman, and more, I felt a lot better about what lies ahead.

No matter the number of *opportunities* you receive as a first sergeant, you can draw upon your past experiences. You might be a mother, father, husband, wife, brother, sister, friend, and much more. Draw upon your experiences to help you care for your Airmen and advise your commander. And with each problem you encounter and resolve, your confidence will grow. Though you might never say you have learned everything there is to know about being a first sergeant, your past experiences can serve as a great foundation in the days and weeks ahead.

2

KNOW
THYSELF

It is important that you understand yourself. You will need to understand who you are and why you do the things you do, as well as any physical, mental, and emotional strengths and weaknesses. The more you know about yourself, the better you can protect yourself from burnout and physical, mental, or emotional breakdowns.

Your first sergeant duty will probably expose things you are good at...*and not so good at.* Some first sergeants love interacting with Airmen but are horrible with administrative tasks. Many might become mentally tired if they address too many issues in a given day, and will need to take a short break, delegate tasks, leave early, or engage in something relaxing when they get home.

During your first sergeant duty, you might also face something that challenges your personal beliefs. The mere thought of the issue will make you angry or cause your hair to stand on end. But in these moments, it is important to address your personal concerns privately and remember why you are a first sergeant.

Each Airman deserves to be treated with dignity and respect—regardless of what he or she has done or believe. You are in the unit to help Airmen, not to lead with your emotions and personal beliefs. You lead with responsible behaviors that internalize our Air Force Core Values and The Airman's Creed. This is what you owe each Airman, and it is what they expect from you. If you are unable to do this, you should reconsider your role as a first sergeant.

3

ENERGY MANAGEMENT

In addition to knowing yourself, you must also pay attention to your energy level. There might come a time when you have to address several negative issues in a row. But if you do not pay attention to how these situations are affecting your physical, mental, or emotional well-being, you might become angry, stressed, or worse...

Unlike the Energizer Bunny, first sergeants do not run on unlimited battery power. If you face a number of negative issues at once or a very significant issue, you might need to take a few moments to recharge, reset, and refocus. To take care of Airmen and be at the top of your game, you must first take care of yourself. Know when you need to sit on the sidelines and take a timeout. Getting out of the office for lunch, taking a day (or more) of leave, and spending time with your family are good ways to help you keep your energy level high.

4

SUPPORT CADRE

Though you might be in a one-deep position, you do not have to do it all alone. Empower your unit Airmen and additional duty first sergeants to help you accomplish specific tasks and responsibilities. Delegating these items will give you the help you need while developing the leadership abilities of your unit Airmen.

Allow your additional duty first sergeants to take on unit issues when you are in the office so they can build their experience and confidence for the times you are not around. But make sure you select the *right* Airmen. Some Airmen need opportunities to excel while others require additional grooming before stepping up. There are also Airmen who might be nosy gossips or power hungry. Choosing the *wrong* Airman will only bring further problems for yourself and the unit.

Right Airman.
Right time.
Right situation.

5

TWO EARS AND ONE MOUTH

It has been said that because you were given two ears and one mouth, you should listen twice as much as you speak. These words cannot be truer for first sergeants. Some Airmen will come to your office to vent, tell their side of the story, and share their lives with you. Give them the opportunity to be heard.

Taking the time to listen to the concerns of your Airmen allow you to understand their perspective and learn what is important to them. Many problems can often be resolved because you learned the *why* of their actions and situation. It helps you get to the root of a problem rather than focusing on symptoms.

Listening twice as much as you speak requires patience. You will need patience when dealing with Airmen, outside agencies, and even your unit and wing leadership. But if you become quick to speak, slow to listen, and quick to become angry, you can quickly lose your credibility, influence, and ability to get things done in a timely manner. A calm message will be better received than one filled with anger.

Listen before you speak.

6

PERSONAL
INTEGRITY

Personal integrity is the hallmark of a first sergeant's character and position. You are expected to be the pillar of Air Force standards. Your position of responsibility and trust requires a high level of integrity, and it can all be lost through one careless act. There are many ways you can maintain personal integrity, but I would like to share four important points:

1. *Do not gossip!* There are few things worse than a gossiping first sergeant. Airmen that come to your office to share personal issues should not have to hear about your conversation from any other Airmen in the unit or across the base. Yes, there are times when

you need to up-channel information, but random gossip just for the sake of it? *No!*

2. *Do not lie!* Be honest and upfront with your commander and your Airmen. If you make a mistake, own up to it rather than blaming someone else.

3. *Love your Airmen, but do not love on your Airmen.* Just because an Airman shows you a bit of attention, it does not mean he or she wants to have an intimate relationship with you. He or she may only be showing respect for your position and expertise. The relationships you have with your unit Airmen should be treated with care, respect, and clear boundaries.

4. *Treat everyone the way you would want to be treated.* This is the Golden Rule! Be respectful and lead with compassion, truth, and Air Force standards. Before you say or do anything, ask yourself how you would feel if someone said or did the same to you.

Regardless of the standards and boundaries you establish, begin and end your first sergeant duty as an Airman of integrity. You do not want your first sergeant duty to be marred with findings of unprofessional relationships or inappropriate behavior.

7

HUMILITY

Nearly all men can stand adversity, but if you want to test a man's character, give him power.

—Abraham Lincoln

As a first sergeant, you are entrusted with a large amount of responsibility and authority. Airmen respect your position. You can get a lot accomplished by simply walking into a room or making a phone call. But just because you have a level of positional power, you should not abuse it through prideful actions and abusive behavior.

As a first sergeant, you are in a position to serve others, not yourself. Do not disrespect yourself, the diamond, or your unit or base Airmen because of a swelling ego. As Uncle Ben told Peter Parker in

Spider-Man, *"With great power comes great responsibility."* You have a tremendous responsibility and tradition to uphold. Be humble. Airmen are counting on you.

8

FLEXIBILITY

First sergeant duty is not Monday through Friday, 0730 to 1630. Your daily focus or planned tasks can change with one phone call, e-mail, or knock on the door. Airmen are not going to wait to call you. When an Airman needs help, he or she will call—*day or night.*

As flexibility is the key to airpower, you must be willing to adjust your schedule for short-notice tasks and issues requiring more immediate attention. If you handle your daily schedule very rigidly, you might break under the stress of your desires to follow a set plan or schedule. However, by handling your daily schedule as a rubber band, you will easily accommodate new meetings, tasks, or issues without a lot of heartache.

Having flexibility at the office is important, but you cannot forget about your family. First sergeant duty is a family affair. It is important that your family understands your new role and responsibilities. Though you take late-night phone calls and weekend responses, your family shares in the frustration, stress, and turmoil of your daily grind and absence from the home.

As you ask your family members to be flexible, you must also be cognizant of their needs. You must care for your family and make time for them as well. Train others and delegate tasks so you can eat dinner with your family, attend your children's activities, and enjoy a vacation or two.

9

TIME
MANAGEMENT

Good time management (coupled with flexibility) will help you manage your responsibilities at home and work. You must be able to prioritize tasks from your commander, wing leadership, and higher headquarters. The hot issue today is replaced with three other hot issues tomorrow.

With so many things that can occur in a first sergeant's day, it is important to have good time management. Some first sergeants block out time in their schedules for specific tasks (e.g., dorm inspections and office visits) and others only focus on top-priority items and leave the rest for *after-hours* and weekends. Create a system that fits your personality and duty requirements.

As first sergeant duty can be extremely demanding, it will be important that you remain focused on your Comprehensive Airman Fitness. Schedule time for your physical wellness, social activities, family, peer, and mentor support, and spiritual health.[1]

---

[1] "Comprehensive Airman Fitness: A Lifestyle and culture," U.S. Air Force, accessed August 3, 2017, http://www.af.mil/News/Article-Display/Article/494434/comprehensive-airman-fitness-a-lifestyle-and-culture/.

10

GOOD ADMINISTRATION AND RECORDS-KEEPING

Having a logical (and simple) way of keeping track of tasks, requests, and other unit and base issues is vitally important. Proper organization can keep you *on point* and focused on your Airmen and mission requirements. As with time management, use a system that works best for you.

Personally, I use both a notebook and Microsoft Outlook to stay on top of tasks, duties, appointments, and meetings. I typically carry a notebook and pen when I am out of the office speaking to Airmen or attending meetings. I will write short notes and memory joggers so I can create calendar appointments, draft e-mails, or further coordinate on tasks and issues when I return to the office.

Within Microsoft Outlook's calendar, I created several color-coded categories that allow me to quickly determine if I have a meeting, awards ceremony, or a first sergeant-specific event. I input tasker and award due dates, personal reminders, and other family appointments. I also share my calendar with my commander and additional duty first sergeants so they can see my daily whereabouts and add to it if necessary.

Proper organization also includes keeping a good system of records. If you start with a good foundation, records-keeping will be much easier to maintain in the months and years ahead, rather than trying to fix things halfway through your tenure.

In Microsoft Outlook, I create Outlook Data Files (PST) for each month—*I save everything!* By dividing my e-mails by month, I can quickly find pertinent items and keep my PST file sizes low if I need to transfer them to a writable disk.

For all official correspondence (including e-mails), you will need to build a system of records. If you are not a records management guru, speak to a records expert in your unit or the Base Records Manager for a bit of guidance and training. If you do nothing, your files will be a mess, and that is not something you want to leave the next first sergeant.

11

RESEARCH AND
ASK FOR HELP

When Airmen see your diamond, they often assume you have all the answers. But if you do not know something, be honest and let your Airmen know that you will find the answer for them. A good Airman does not need to know every answer...*just where to find it.* And when you find the answer, you can act as if you are the subject matter expert like most first sergeants do.

Outside of your own personal knowledge and experiences, there are four other sources of help and support:

1. *First sergeant's council.* Your first sergeant's council is filled with a wealth of knowledge and

experience. They are your brothers and sisters in arms who experience similar challenges and successes. Most councils create continuity books or have a shared drive with useful documents and guidance.

2. *Google.* There is a wealth of information on the Internet. If you do not know what the EPR AFI might be, conduct an Internet search. The answer you are looking for might be one of the first results.

3. *Support agencies.* Build rapport with support agencies through personal visits, responsive support, and a pleasant demeanor. Using *please* and *thank you* and acknowledging good work and quick responses go a long way in building relationships.

4. *Personnel programs (i.e., BLSDM, PRDA, AMS).* Obtain access to these systems and take the time to understand how they work and how they can benefit you and your Airmen. If you do not have any personnelists in your unit, visit your MPF to learn about these programs firsthand. You can also supplement your training with Personnel Services Delivery Memorandums on myPers and other locally-developed materials.

12

LEADING FROM THE FRONT OR THE REAR

Being a first sergeant is not a spectator sport. You will need to be proactive and anticipate questions that might come from your commander and wing leadership. When an incident occurs, you should try to gather as much information as possible (*who, what, why, when, where, and how*) before speaking with your commander. More than likely, your commander will need to report the same information to his or her boss. If your notification is time-sensitive and cannot wait, let your commander know what information you have and your next steps.

When it comes to specific processes and procedures, take the time to read policies and AFI references and speak to subject matter experts. This is often for your own situational awareness and growth, but they can also be helpful for your commander. You want to ensure he or she is armed with the best information available to make an informed decision. Now, some commanders might not want a lot of background information, but that does not excuse your need to research and prepare yourself.

13

GATEKEEPER

As a first sergeant, you have the ability, authority, and responsibility to either do the right thing or do things right on behalf of your Airmen. And this begins with your commander.

I am extremely watchful and protective of my commander's signature and time. I try to decrease foot traffic, adjust administrative workflow processes, and add *blocked* time to his calendar so he can focus on administrative work and other tasks. If there is a decision that he does not have to make, I will make it for him (after prior coordination) or delegate it to someone else who can. Commanders are people too.

I also do not allow my unit Airmen to submit documents for the commander's coordination or signature without background information. If an Airman wants the commander to sign his or her reenlistment documents, he or she should provide a copy of his or her fitness score sheet and last three EPRs. Also, if an Airman is submitting any other correspondence, he or she should provide as much information as possible for the commander to make an informed decision. Make sure your Airmen do their homework.

Lastly, use your voice, authority, and position to take care of your Airmen. You have a seat at the table of many leadership discussions. Listen and provide your input and perspective when appropriate, but do not abuse your invitations. Be the voice your Airmen need to properly balance programs, processes, and personnel decisions.

14

FOLLOW UP

Nothing is better than seeing an empty to-do list (if that even exists). But a first sergeant's work is hardly ever done. As much as you would like to complete your checklist, you will need to engage your Airmen and support agencies on a consistent basis to ensure they are making progress on specific issues or simply as a wellness check.

Whether you have a to-do list, a spreadsheet matrix, or some other system, ensure that you have something in place to remind you of Airmen and unit issues and other situations on your commander's radar. You will often *score* a lot of points with Airmen for remembering their situations and checking on them from time to time. (Remember to engage the

Airman's supervisor and leadership chain as well.) Plus, your commander will appreciate periodic updates on issues that have reached his or her level.

15

COMMANDER INTENT

Your position as a first sergeant is not meant for you to *do your own thing* every day. You answer to your unit and your commander. Therefore, it is important that you understand your commander's vision, command philosophy, and expectations for the unit, as well as his or her intent, direction, and guidance for you.

Sometimes, your commander's intent is very clear, and at other times, it is implied. For example, your commander might say, *"I want that Airman gone as soon as possible!"* Your commander has given his or her intent, and you should make it your business to ensure that the Airman is out of the military as soon as possible without breaking any AFIs or local laws.

There will also be times when you will not agree with a decision your commander makes. Now, this is not the time to argue with your commander or burn any bridges over the issue. When you disagree, take a moment or a day or two to consider your position as well as your commander's. Then return to him or her to discuss your position once more (maybe armed with more information). Some first sergeants even ask their commanders for three opportunities (or strikes) to present their concerns. But once your commander has made his or her final decision, and his or her door opens, salute smartly and support your commander's decision. It will be detrimental to go against your commander's decision in word or deed (especially in front of other Airmen).

16

STICKING
TO THE SCRIPT

In sticking to the script, it is important to advise your commander through the myriad of unit meetings and issues. Many commanders want to share their personal thoughts and frustrations during the Article 15 process, discharges, and other administrative actions (and it is his or her right to do so). But sometimes, less is more.

A few years ago, during my first Article 15 as an additional duty first sergeant, the commander told the Airman that he did not believe the Airman had committed the acts that he was being accused of. Then when the chief brought the Airman and me into his office, he repeated the same thing. I was confused and shocked. So when the Airman asked me for my thoughts, I told him I was not in a position to provide my personal opinion, and he should speak with his Area Defense Council. However, the commander continued with the Article 15.

A few days after the Article 15 was completed, I met with the commander and told him to never to say anything like that again. He was shocked that I said it, but I learned a valuable lesson in the process. I realized the importance of a *pregame* message to ensure that the commander (and everyone present) is advised on what should occur in a specific meeting. I should make sure everyone involved remains within acceptable boundaries of communication and conduct.

Now, some commanders will do or say whatever they want, regardless of your counsel, perspective, or opinion. Just remember you are in a position to advise, not to force your opinion. Do not take these situations personally.

As a first sergeant, it should be your hope to help your commander enjoy a successful command without being fired or landing in jail. So *pregame* your meetings and discussions to ensure your commander sticks to the script.

17

INFORMATION FOR THE MASSES

First sergeants receive countless e-mails each week about base events, tasks, and other useful information. If you send each message individually, you might quickly disinterest your Airmen. As soon as they see your name in their inboxes, they will press *delete*. But I would like to suggest a different approach.

If you receive time-sensitive or burning-hot messages, please send them judiciously, but for general information, I recommend consolidating your messages into weekly e-mails.

Each week I send out a Shirt Dirt e-mail.[2] The e-mail typically has the following headings: Shirt Dirt Today (general information), Guidance/Policies, Good to Know, Forms and AFIs, New Links, and Calendar Events. When possible, I try to keep each e-mail under one megabyte in size. Outside of the information I receive from base agencies, I review several Air Force websites and social media pages to collect other pertinent news and information. I create hyperlinks to specific web pages and attach as few items as possible. I also include a mix of financial, fitness, and other personal and professional tips, tools, and guidance from around the Internet.

---

[2] Shirt Dirt originated from SMSgt Ryan Hutchison, who was my first sergeant shortly before I became a first sergeant in 2012.

18

SAVE BAD NEWS
FOR MONDAY

When your commander has an LOR, Article 15, discharge notification, or some other adverse action to serve an Airman, and it happens to be Friday, save it for Monday. Delivering adverse actions and punishments on Fridays can manifest into significant problems over the weekend.

Saturday and Sunday provide a lot of time for an Airman to think about what has occurred. He or she can quickly turn to heavy drinking, suicidal thoughts, or worse. But issuing disciplinary action Monday through Thursday might provide you time to closely monitor the Airman's behavior and send him or her to the appropriate support agency if needed.

Now, this is not a *catch-all* for preventing all negative reactions to adverse actions, but you can at least mitigate some issues. Regardless of when your commander chooses to discipline an Airman or share negative information, ensure the Airman's supervisor (or someone from their leadership chain) is present and engaged with the Airman throughout the situation.

19

ALL ABOUT PEOPLE

Remember: Your job is people. As you continue as a first sergeant, do not lose sight of the person behind the name tag standing in front of you. You can deal with so many issues that you begin to make decisions on *autopilot,* without compassion or remembering that your Airmen are people too.

If you are not careful, your heart can harden to the cares and concerns of your Airmen, and you will miss the true reason why you are a first sergeant. People are your business—not only disciplining them but also building them back up.

The resilience of some Airmen will be completely shattered as they face significant work or family situations. You are a pillar of help and support in their hour of need. Airmen come to you when they need help, and when their resiliency returns, they will move on. But the impact you can make in their lives will continue long after your assignment in the unit.

20

PAYBACK

First sergeants serve in a special position that few will experience in their military careers. We share a unique fellowship and encounter many of the same struggles and successes. And as such, we should be able to relate to one another and be a source of comfort, camaraderie, and support when needed.

So whether you serve as a first sergeant for one tenure or more, lend your knowledge and support to your fellow first sergeants. Maybe you can be the council *mom* or *dad*, take new first sergeants under your wing, or host a social event. But how you choose to serve your fellow first sergeants can be as unique as your personality. Work within your passion and allow it to propel your service to other first sergeants.

CONCLUSION

I hope your time as a first sergeant will become one of the most rewarding of your military career. You are a part of a unique cadre of Airmen called to serve and support other Airmen on a daily basis.

I also hope these twenty *essentials* will be a great benefit to you. I encourage you to share them with your first sergeant's council and additional duty first sergeants. Add to these essentials and make them your own. They were created with you in mind—to help you grow and succeed.

(com)mission
PUBLISHING

www.commissionpubs.com
info@commissionpubs.com

www.ingramcontent.com/pod-product-compliance
Lightning Source LLC
Chambersburg PA
CBHW071645040426
42452CB00009B/1772